BODY IMAGE

BEAUTY

STANDARDS

AND

SELF

CONFIDENCE

FOR GIRLS AND WOMEN

Lizeth May Daniels

~ 1 ~

TABLE OF CONTENTS

CHAPTER SIX

INTRODUCTION

We now live in a world where how you look or appear to a person defines you. Somehow how you look or people's perception of your body is the deciding factor on how they relate with you and regard you. Society or people choose to put you in a prison of their own choosing based on what their ideal type is and the irony of it all is that they are so indecisive about what their ideal type is. They could term you beautiful today and not tomorrow. It is also normal to see a skinny person being shamed for being too skinny and a fatter person belittled also for eating too much. They seem to have something to say nevertheless. If you have ever experienced bullying or more because of your size, color, face or any other thing in regards to your body image, you are not alone- but you are more than your size, you are more than your appearance. Do not let someone else's offhand remark mess with you or make you feel less than you really are. You and you alone should choose how to treat your body, value and respect it.

How frequently do you search in the mirror and say "On the off chance that I could simply shed ten pounds, then, at that point, I could be blissful"?

Sadly, most of American ladies and young ladies are disappointed with their bodies, and many go to outrageous lengths trying to change their bodies. For instance, one investigation discovered that 63% of female members recognized load as the vital calculate deciding how they had an outlook on themselves - more significant than family, school, or vocation. Other examination proposes that 86% of all ladies are disappointed with their bodies and need to get thinner. Ladies and juvenile young ladies respect size, similar as weight, as a conclusive component of their personality. A few young ladies expect something isn't quite right about their bodies when they can't fit predictably into some "standard" size; others will dismiss some pants just in light of the fact that they won't wear a specific size. Most of young ladies step on the scale to decide their self-esteem; on the off chance that they have shed pounds, it is a decent day and they can momentarily feel "OK" about themselves. In the event that the number on the scale has expanded somewhat, the day is demolished and they feel useless. Self-perception has now become interwoven with one's weight, and hence, in the event that ladies are not content with their weight, they can not in any way, shape or form happy with their bodies. Sadly, young ladies and women take this a stride farther and support that negative self-perception is straightforwardly compared to mental self view. We are presently residing in a general public where little kids trust the one approach to work on their mental self view and to feel more certain is to shed pounds and become more slender.

Ladies and little kids are presently residing in a general public where their bodies characterize what their identity is. Young ladies are frightened to put on weight and are persistently reminded by the media about different new eating routine items available, and the worth in weight reduction. They are likewise besieged by endless TV programs on plastic medical procedure and the quantity of corrective medical procedures in the world are expanding consistently. Ladies today face unimaginable pictures of beauty consistently when they sit in front of the TV, see a film, or view a magazine. It is assessed that little kids are presented to 400 to 600 media pictures each day. Little kids and ladies unpreventably have an unreliable outlook on their bodies and actual appearance and frequently accept they should change their bodies to acquire confidence. A new review saw that as just 2% of ladies on the planet would depict themselves as "lovely." by far most of young ladies need to change different parts of their appearance. In the present society, confidence and body-regard have become very much the same. Sadly this is having a profound cost for little kids, and they are feeling deficient and frequently go to extreme ways of behaving trying to control their bodies to "fit into" a ridiculous norm of excellence. Dietary problems have prospered in this beauty driven society. Little kids and ladies are caught in a negative pattern of body scorn. Ladies with dietary issues are especially defenseless against this negative self-perception cycle.

Albeit a larger part of ladies are disappointed with their bodies, numerous women and young ladies experience outrageous self-perception troubles that can be important for additional muddled issues. These outrageous self-perception unsettling influences incorporate body dysmorphic jumble, dietary issues and serious wretchedness.

CHAPTER ONE

What is body image?

Body image is the insight that an individual has of their physical appearance, yet more critically the considerations and sentiments the individual encounters because of that discernment. It is essential to comprehend that these sentiments can be positive, negative or a mix of both and it can be impacted by the individual and other factors.

For what reason is positive self-perception significant? Individuals with positive self-perception will by and large have a more elevated level of physical and mental wellbeing, and better self-improvement. A good self-perception will impact:

- A good self regard or esteem levels: Self regard is how an individual feels about themselves and this can invade each part of such individual's reality. The higher your confidence, the more amiable you will be, prompting more elevated levels of bliss and satisfaction.

- Self-acknowledgment: The more good an individual's self-perception, the more probable that individual is to feel great and content with the manner in which they look. An individual with good self-perception is less inclined to feel influenced by unreasonable pictures in the media and cultural tensions to look a specific way.
- Healthy viewpoint and ways of behaving: When you are on top of, and answer the requirements of your body, your physical and mental prosperity moves along. A positive self-perception will prompt a decent way of life with better perspectives and practices with food and exercise.

What causes body disappointment?

At the point when an individual has pessimistic contemplations and sentiments about their own body, body disappointment begins to creep in. Society assumes a huge part in how individuals see and feel about their body. An individual's family, companions, colleagues, educators and the media all affect how that individual sees and feels about themselves and their appearance. Specifically, when an individual is in an environment where one's appearance is taken too seriously or gets negative criticism about their appearance, for instance, by being prodded, they are at an expanded gamble of body disappointment. Individuals of any age are barraged with pictures through media like TV, magazines, web and promoting. These pictures are frequently ridiculous, hopeless and profoundly stylized and filtered, advancing beauty and appearance standards for guys and females in our general public. They send solid messages which reaffirm that in our way of life flimsy is delightful for females and lean/strong is the ideal body shape for guys and that when these body shapes are accomplished that joy, achievement and love will result. The ideal exhibited in these pictures has been manufactured by beauticians, workmanship groups and computerized control and cannot be made or accomplished, in actuality. On the off chance that an individual feels that they do not gauge up in contrast with these pictures, sensations of body disappointment can heighten and damagingly affect that individual's mental health and self esteem.

Although some individuals are bound to foster a negative self-perception than others. This can be as consequence of the accompanying elements:

- Age - self-perception issues can influence individuals from youth across the life expectancy and are as common in midlife as youthful adulthood in ladies. Notwithstanding, convictions about self-perception are regularly formed during late youth and puberty so this is an especially urgent time.

- Gender - young ladies are more inclined to self-perception disappointment than young men; but the paces of body disappointment in guys is quickly moving toward that of females

- People who experience low confidence as well as depression.

- Personality qualities - individuals with stickler propensities (for example individuals who feel a requirement for everything in their lives to be great), successful people and individuals who intellectually are more 'high contrast' in their reasoning, the individuals who assimilate and esteem beauty standards, and individuals who will generally contrast themselves with others, are at higher gamble of creating body disappointment

- Appearance prodding - individuals who are prodded for their appearance, particularly weight, paying little mind to genuine appearance or weight, are at a more serious gamble of developing body disappointment than the individuals who are not.

- Having loved ones who diet for weight reduction and express high self-perception concerns - when an individual is in a climate in which focal individuals express self-perception concerns and model weight reduction ways of behaving, they are bound to foster body disappointment themselves paying little heed to real appearance or weight

A portion of the elements that add to a negative self-perception include:

- being prodded about appearance in adolescence
- experiencing childhood in a family where accentuation is put on appearance of a specific ideal body size or shape
- Guardians and other relatives encountering body disappointment and participating in eating fewer carbs or weight control ways of behaving
- A social propensity to pass judgment on individuals by their appearance
- peer tension among high schoolers or young ladies to be thin, stop eating so much junk

food, exercise and contrast themselves to other people

- Media and publicizing pictures that advance specific appearance beliefs
- A propensity in ladies' media to push trend diets and get-healthy plans
- Benevolent general wellbeing efforts that urge individuals to get in shape.
- Glow up and infantilization culture on social media

Body Dysmorphia

This is an issue of "envisioned grotesqueness." What people with this problem find in the mirror is a horribly contorted perspective on what they really resemble. Frequently, these people will go through hours analyzing, endeavoring to cover, or fixating on their apparent defects. Certain individuals really burn through a large number of dollars on plastic medical procedure trying to work on their bodies.

Anorexia Nervosa: This problem is described by an intense apprehension about putting on weight and these people really see their bodies as bigger or "fat" despite the fact that they are horribly underweight.

Bulimia Nervosa: People with this issue are likewise exceptionally disappointed with their bodies and have intense worry with body weight and shape.

Melancholy: In many cases, people with melancholy frequently have a twisted perspective on themselves and accept they are less appealing than they truly are.

Since negative self-perception is a pervasive issue for some women and young ladies and can likewise be a part of numerous serious problems, it is important that ladies figure out how to change their self-perception towards a solid and positive perspective on self.

CHAPTER TWO

Seven Methods for defeating Negative Self-perception

1. Battle "Fatism"

Work on tolerating individuals of all sizes and shapes. This will assist you with valuing your own body. It could be helpful to make a rundown of individuals you respect that don't have "great" bodies. Does their appearance influence how you feel about them? It is likewise vital to recall that society's guidelines have changed altogether throughout recent years. The ladies that were viewed as the ideal beauties in earlier years were full-bodied and genuinely gorgeous ladies, yet they would be thought of "overweight" by the present principles.

2. Battle the Eating regimen Ruin

A lot of ladies have slimmed down sooner or later in their life, and at the particular moment, half of ladies are eating less junk food. A new overview saw that as 14% of five-year old young ladies report that they "start a new and improved eating routine" trying to shed pounds. When young ladies are a decade old, 80% report holding off on junk food. Ladies are twice bound to slim down than men. Research has found that when controlled eaters are presented to plugs connected with diet, weight reduction, or wellness, they experience pessimistic feelings and are bound to then indulge. Ladies are absurd assuming they accept that consuming less calories will help them have an improved outlook on themselves. Eating less junk food just assists you with losing your confidence and energy. Counting calories likewise makes temperament swings and sensations of sadness. To battle the eating regimen destruction, an instinctive eating approach can be very useful. This approach centers around control of a wide range of food sources and not including calories or mark perusing. Food is "just food" and not marked as "great" or "terrible." Clients figure out how to screen their craving/completion and partake in a solid relationship with food. In the event that you feel strain to shed pounds, converse with a companion or cherished one, or look for proficient assistance. There are numerous useful books that emphasis on instinctive eating that might be a decent asset.

3. Acknowledge Hereditary qualities

It is basic to recall that numerous parts of your body can't be changed. Hereditary qualities assume a part in your body and something like 25% to 70% of your body is not entirely settled by your qualities. While there are numerous parts of your body we can't transform, you can change or adjust your convictions and perspectives which impact the manner in which you feel about yourself. Change begins with you - it is interior, and it begins with dignity and an inspirational perspective. Zeroing in on wellbeing and not size is significant. It is critical to not contrast your body and your companions, relatives, or media pictures. We are interesting, and no two bodies are something similar. We can't be really blissful or healthy if we "diet into" another body.

4. Comprehend that Feelings are Shallow

It is essential to find the feelings and sentiments that underlie your pessimistic self-perception. The assertion "I feel fat" is rarely truly about fat, regardless of whether you are overweight. Each time a lady checks out herself in the mirror and says "Gross, I'm fat and sickening," she is truly saying "Something is off about me or with what I'm feeling." When we don't have the foggiest idea how to manage our sentiments we go to our bodies and fault our bodies for our sentiments. Each time you say "I'm fat" you are deceiving your body and you are selling out and disregarding your basic sentiments. Recollect that "fat" is never an inclination; it's evasion of sentiments. Figure out how to find your feelings and sentiments, and understand that zeroing in on your body is just diverting you based on the thing is "truly" irritating you.

5. Question Messages Depicted in the Media

The media sends strong messages to young ladies and women about the adequacy (or inadmissibility) of their bodies. Little kids are educated to contrast themselves with ladies depicted as effective in the media, surveying how intently they coordinate to the "ideal" body structure. Sadly, most of young ladies and women do not coordinate to the models and entertainers introduced in the media. The typical model is 5'11" and weighs 117 pounds, though the normal ladies is 5'3/8" and weighs 166.2 pounds. This is the biggest inconsistency that has at any point existed among ladies and the social ideal. This error leads numerous ladies and young ladies to have an insufficient and negative outlook on their bodies. It is critical to understand that just 1.8% of ladies hereditarily have the "ideal" body right now introduced in the media. The other 98.2% of ladies feel they should go above and beyond to endeavor to arrive at this absurd picture. A significant number of the pictures introduced in the media have been PC upgraded and enhanced with filters. The models' hips and midsections have frequently been thinned and their bosoms augmented through PC photograph control. Large numbers of the ladies introduced in the media experience the ill effects of a dietary problem or have taken on scattered eating ways of behaving to keep up with such low body size. It means quite a bit to begin to address pictures in the media and question why ladies ought to feel a sense of urgency to "live up" to these unreasonable norms of beauty and slenderness.

One fascinating side note: Once beauty magazine attempted to utilize more "normal size" models in their magazine and found that deals went down. It is fascinating that exploration exhibits that ladies report having an uplifting perspective on their bodies subsequent to seeing typical pictures of ladies in the media; however this did not further develop readership for the magazine.

6. Perceive the Impact of Body Misperception

Ladies are inclined to additional gloomy sentiments about their bodies than men. By and large, ladies all the more mentally put resources into their actual appearance. Your self-perception is key to how you feel about yourself. Research uncovers that as much as 1/4 of your confidence is the aftereffect of how positive or negative your self-perception is. Tragically, numerous ladies with dietary issues have a bigger level of their regard put resources into their bodies. Ladies with dietary problems frequently display unequivocal self-perception misperception, in which they misperceive the size of part, or the whole body. Subsequently they are "visually impaired" to their own figures. This bending is genuine and it isn't because of "fat," yet to the dietary problem disease. It is vital to perceive this misperception and characterize it to the dietary problem. At the point when you feel fat, advise yourself that you misperceive your shape. Judge your size as per the assessments of trusted acquaintances until you can trust your new and more precise self-insights.

7. Become a close acquaintance with Your Body

It is vital to battle negative self-perception since it can prompt sorrow, timidity, social uneasiness and hesitance in close connections. Negative self-perception may likewise prompt a dietary issue. It is time that ladies quit passing judgment on their bodies cruelly and figure out how to see the value in their inward being. A ladies' body is more than just its size or appearance, it is so special it can even make life. Begin to remember you don't need to contrast yourself with different ladies in the media. Start to challenge pictures introduced in the media, and understand that your value doesn't rely heavily on how intently you fit these ridiculous pictures.

Learn to adore and value your body.

Here are instances of 10 different ways you can adore your body:

1. Affirm there's nothing that can be done about it.
2. Think of your body as an instrument. Make a stock of the multitude of things you can do with it.
3. Walk with your head high with satisfaction and trust in yourself personally, not a size.
4. Create a rundown of individuals you respect who have added to your life, your local area, or the world. Was their appearance critical to their prosperity and achievements?
5. Don't let your size hold you back from doing things you appreciate.

6. Replace the time you enjoy censuring your appearance with additional positive, fulfilling pursuits.
7. Let your internal excellence and distinction sparkle.
8. Think back to a period in your life when you loved and partook in your body. Reach out to those sentiments now.
9. Be your body's partner and promoter, not its foe.
10. Beauty isn't simply shallow. It is an impression of your entire self. Love and partake in the individual inside.

CHAPTER THREE

Social Media Is a Toxic Mirror

We've long perceived that motion pictures, magazines and TV harm youngsters' self-perception by upholding a "slim ideal."

Social media has likewise turned into a harmful mirror.

Recently, therapists found powerful culturally diverse proof connecting social media use to body image concerns, eating fewer carbs, body reconnaissance, a drive for slenderness and self-generalization in teenagers.

 Note: that doesn't mean online entertainments cause the issues, yet that there's serious areas of strength from them.

Visual stages like Facebook, Instagram and Snapchat convey the devices that permit youngsters to procure endorsement for their appearance and contrast themselves with others. The weakest clients, scientists say, are the ones who invest the vast majority of their energy posting, remarking on and contrasting themselves with photographs. One investigation discovered that female undergrads who did this on Facebook were bound to connect their self-esteem to their looks. Strangely, while young ladies report more self-perception aggravation and confused eating than young men — studies have shown both can be similarly harmed by online entertainment.

Furthermore, because of a variety of free applications, selfie-holics now have the ability to change their bodies in pictures such that's essentially comparable to cosmetics and other beauty items. Youngsters can conceal pimples, brighten teeth and even digitally embellish with the swipe of a finger, organizing their own picture to become prettier, more slender and hotter. All this gives a deception of control: on the off chance that I invest more energy and truly work at it, I can improve at being lovely. "In the event that I would be able, my body would appear to be unique. However, I can pick which picture makes my arms look more slender."

Yet, constantly, the line between a "like" and feeling positioned becomes obscure. It influences adolescents subliminally simply perceiving the number of preferences they that stand out enough to be noticed get only for what they look like.

What youngsters share online is overshadowed by what they consume. Pre-Internet, you needed to get going to the supermarket to find a magazine with big name bodies — or possibly filch your mom's duplicate from the washroom. Presently the photos are however unending as they seem to be accessible. Youngsters can go through hours focusing on the conditioned arms or glutes of famous people, who peddle their bodies as much as their ability.

The transient ascent of the "health" industry online has sent off a whole industry of wellness famous people via web-based entertainment. A huge number of devotees embrace their regimens for diet and exercise, however progressively, the drive for "wellbeing" and "clean eating" has become secretive cover for seriously counting calories and hardship. This year, an investigation of 50 supposed "fitspiration" sites uncovered informing that was undefined, on occasion, from supportive of anorexia or "thinspiration" sites. Both contained coarse speech initiating responsibility about weight or the body, and advanced eating fewer carbs, restriction and fat and weight derision.

Numerous teenagers are media-proficient about films and magazines; they take in carefully changed pictures with a basic eye. Most teenagers disregard discussions about the hazards of social media with a "duh" or "I know that generally." That doesn't mean they're not tuning in, or feeling stressed that their bodies don't have the right stuff.

Virtual entertainment and social media can attack your self-perception

Continually contrasting yourself with pictures of big names or powerhouses can make you have a negative self-perception.

- Virtual entertainment can adversely influence self-perception by over-presenting you to "glorified" body types.
- While posting selfies might assist with self perception, attempting to alter out apparent imperfections can be hurtful in the long run.
- To decrease hurt via social media, unfollow some certain accounts and enjoy reprieves.

With an expected 3.9 billion users around the world, virtual entertainment is an enormous piece of the present culture. Yet, reliably looking at posts —

especially pictures that inspire gloomy sentiments or lift a specific body type — can influence how you see yourself.

Since online entertainment is loaded up with individuals introducing themselves in their best light, it very well may be hard to keep away from pictures and messages that could cause you to feel adversely about your body. In any case, there are ways you can organize your feed to set aside a better room for you.

What social media can adversely mean for self-perception

Self-perception alludes to your viewpoint of your body's appearance and the way that it conforms to cultural guidelines. A negative self-perception can cause ridiculous assumptions for how your body ought to look and could prompt undesirable ways of behaving, as disarranged eating.

A little 2018 review figured out a relationship between's opportunity spent via virtual entertainment, negative self-perception, and disarranged eating. This was particularly evident on the off chance that members were looking at appearance-related content, similar to the record of a health specialist or model on Instagram.

Here are the subtle ways that online entertainment can twist how you see your body:

1. Comparing yourself with others

One of the manners in which virtual entertainment can hurt your self-perception is by presenting you to pictures of "glorified" body types, making you contrast yourself with them.

Individuals wind up making ridiculous beliefs for themselves in view of what they see and feel troubled when they can't meet those thoughts or self-assumptions.

Young ladies who invest more energy on instagram or tiktok might have a more concerned outlook on their body since they contrast their appearance with others (particularly to peers). These examinations can be essential for an endless loop.

The more you contrast yourself with individuals you follow via virtual entertainment, the more disappointed you become with your bodies. Also, assuming you are already disappointed with how you look, it could expand the drive to contrast yourself with others via virtual entertainment.

This conduct could prompt confused eating or other unfortunate things to do. Each sort of dietary issue has various side effects, however a few indications of a dietary problem can include:

- Low body weight
- Successive weight variances
- Concealing food or eating alone
- Distraction with body weight or appearance
- Gorging then vomiting

If you figure you might have a dietary issue, converse with a specialist or psychological wellness proficient who can assist you with seeking treatment and track down a way to recuperation.

2. Photoshop and filters

Of all the photographs you see on your virtual entertainment, there's a decent opportunity the majority of them have been altered. Almost 66% of Americans alter their photographs prior to posting.

Photoshop and filters that adjust or alter pictures can likewise add to negative self-perception.

Photoshop and filters present individuals and things in their best light. It makes a contorted dreamland and increases present expectations on what individuals see is 'the most effective' way to be.

Indeed, even the most common way of altering your own pictures can assume a part of the way you see your body. In fact it has been proven that taking and altering selfies was more harmful than posting them, maybe in light of the fact that it permits you to zero in on — and attempt to fix — your blemishes.

3. Fitspo and thinspo

Fitspiration and thinspiration — also called "fitspo" and "thinspo" — are terms that portray online entertainment records and pictures that urge clients to be fit and slim.

Analysts inferred that additional time spent on social media prompts more incessant body and weight examinations and more gloomy sentiments around one's body. It additionally found that for ladies who needed to get thinner, additional time on social media brought about more disarranged eating side effects.

4. Adverse consequences for men

While most examinations via virtual entertainment and self-perception center around ladies, a recent report tracked down comparative impacts in men.

The review examined 1,000 Instagram posts transferred by male-distinguishing people and assessed reactions — as preferences and remarks. The greater part of the posts portrayed strength and leanness, and the posts showing this body type got the largest number of preferences and remarks. The scientists presumed that these discoveries are "possibly hurtful to men's self-perception."

For men, the expansion of a fit, muscle-loaded body type via virtual entertainment could prompt body disappointment and muscle dysmorphia. Muscle dysmorphia — a sort of body dysmorphia — is the point at which one sees that their body isn't solid or inclined enough. It can make individuals participate in undesirable measures of activity and may prompt scattered eating.

As indicated by a 2015 report, marks of shame around looking for help for dysfunctional behavior and dietary issues could deter a few men from seeking a finding and treatment. Also, the supposition that ladies are generally impacted by dietary problems could make more men go undiscovered and less inclined to get treatment almost immediately, when it would be best.

How virtual entertainment and social media can advance body image

Adverse consequences of virtual entertainment on self-perception are legitimate, however social media can likewise emphatically affect your self-perception.

1. Body positive contents and networks

Body positive content tries to show appreciation and acknowledgment for a wide range of bodies. Analysts reasoned that in the wake of review good satisfied, the ladies rested easier thinking about their bodies, yet they were likewise feeling better.

Individuals will generally copy what they see or change their assumptions for themselves in light of what others are doing or what they look like. Promoters of body positivity and compelling figures certainly have a one of a kind capacity to have a beneficial outcome on how individuals view themselves and their bodies, particularly with regards to youngsters.

Social media can likewise decidedly influence self-perception by interfacing you with others that assist with building a body-tolerating community.

2. Instagram versus reality

One pattern that means to uncover online entertainment's ultra-organized, performative norms are "Instagram versus reality" pictures. These pictures frequently show an altered photograph of somebody at their best point close by a more "genuine" photograph that shows their defects.

In a recent report, ladies were shown these sorts of posts, either in their unique structure or simply the "truth" or "instagram" pictures independently. Analysts found that ladies felt less disappointment with their bodies subsequent to seeing either the "truth" pictures or the "instagram versus reality" pictures one next to the other.

Tips to encourage a solid relationship with virtual entertainment

Virtual entertainment can adversely influence your self-perception, state of mind, and generally psychological well-being, yet there are ways of checking this. The following are three ideas for organizing a more sure feed:

1. Enjoy some time off.
   In the event that you find you feel more terrible subsequent to looking over, make a stride back and perceive how you feel in the wake of separating. Assuming you feel much improved, there's no disgrace in

putting your telephone down for some time, whether that be a couple of hours, days, or weeks. Indeed, even a weeklong break can be sufficient to support your mind-set.

2. Unfollow accounts that don't encourage you. Focus on which records, individuals, and pictures lift you up.

3. Track down a local area. Follow body positive communities and join strong gatherings that can assist with moving your outlook about "great" body types.

You might think you are essentially looking at virtual entertainment to loosen up, yet research has found the pictures you see and individuals you connect with can affect your self-discernment.

However, that doesn't mean all virtual entertainment use is terrible. It simply implies you might have to reconsider how you utilize social media.

You can make social media a better climate for you, whether that implies unfollowing certain people and taking a few breaks off the internet every once in a while.

CHAPTER FOUR

What is BDD (Body Dysmorphic Disorder)?

Have you at any point searched in a mirror and become focused on a pimple or a scar or other imperfection that you see on your skin? Or on the other hand have you been consumed by the possibility that your nose looks unusual? Envision imagining that these defects were the main things others saw when they took a gander at you, with these considerations prompting sensations of disgrace, self-loathing, and excessively decisive contemplations about your appearance.

At the point when these contemplations and sentiments become excessively tedious and cause huge close to home pain (like tension, misery, or hesitance) or potentially critical issues in your everyday existence — this is body dysmorphia. Likewise, eventually, individuals with BDD additionally participate in unnecessary dreary enthusiastic ways of behaving (like contrasting themselves with others or unnecessarily taking a look at mirrors or prepping) because of their appearance concerns.

Body dysmorphic jumble (BDD), likewise called body dysmorphia, is an emotional well-being condition that includes a staggering distraction with one's body and appearance. Somebody with BDD might zero in exorbitantly on minor actual defects or stress over apparent imperfections that others don't notice.

What are the normal signs and side effects of BDD?

- Successive considerations about appearance (basically an hour daily).
- Investing a great deal of energy gazing in a mirror while focused on the apparent defect, or at times, complete evasion of mirrors/reflective surfaces.
- Concealing the despised body region (for instance, utilizing caps, scarves, make-up, body position, or stance).
- Over and over inquiring as to whether you look alright (additionally alluded to as 'consolation chasing').

- Incessant meetings with clinical experts/restorative specialists to get the loathed body region "fixed."
- Rehashed plastic medical procedure or dermatologic therapy.
- Enthusiastic skin picking, which incorporates utilizing fingernails and tweezers to eliminate seen imperfections as well as hair.
- Staying away from social circumstances, public spots, work, school, and so forth.
- Going out once in a while or just going out around evening time to keep others from seeing the "imperfection."
- Maintaining your fixations and keeping them secret without asking for help because of sensations of disgrace
- Constant feeling of repugnance, sorrow, nervousness, low confidence, self-destructive reasoning, and so forth.

It is essential to take note of that individuals living with BDD look "typical." The appearance defects that they see are, in all actuality, negligible or nonexistent. Notwithstanding, the individual with BDD for the most part does not understand this. They imagine that the imperfections show up as revolting to other people, and that they are as perceptible to every other person as they are to themselves. This is presumably on the grounds that individuals with BDD have contrasts in visual handling - they appear to really see themselves uniquely in contrast to others do.

How would you differentiate between being discontent with a piece of your appearance and BDD?

Many individuals are discontent with how a certain part of their body looks; nonetheless, assuming that the time and energy spent contemplating the body part impedes everyday working or causes critical profound trouble, then, at that point, the individual is determined to have BDD.

Many individuals are discontent with some part of the manner in which they look. In any case, you might have BDD if:

1. You spend no less than one hour altogether daily (include constantly you spend) pondering the apparent appearance defects, and
2. Distraction with the apparent imperfections obstructs everyday working or causes depression

3. Eventually you become consumed with negative thoughts and feeling because of the appearance concerns.

Which parts of the body is many times the focal point of BDD?

- Most frequently, the head or face (for example hair, nose, skin break out, neck, and so on) are the focal point of concern. Nonetheless, individuals with BDD can be exorbitantly stressed over any body part.
- Other normal areas of concern incorporate the arms, legs, stomach, hips, weight, and body work (for instance, feeling not muscular or fit enough).

BDD is recorded inside the class of over the top impulsive and related disorders. This implies it includes the two fixations (meddlesome, determined considerations) and impulses (activities that somebody performs more than once trying to decrease anxiety).

Predominance of Body Dysmorphic Issue

A survey suggests that up to 4% of the U.S. populace meets the symptomatic measures for body dysmorphic jumble. It is generally normal among individuals age 15-30. Research says that individuals with BDD frequently go through three to eight hours daily stressing over their apparent actual blemishes. Any body part might turn into an objective for these concerns. Nonetheless, individuals with body dysmorphia are probably going to stress over their skin, nose, or hair.

Somebody with body dysmorphia may feel so consumed with contemplations about their looks that they disregard different aspects of their life. They might try and stay away from school, get-togethers, dating, or work out of dread of being belittled or judged for their looks.

At the point when left untreated, BDD can prompt serious adverse results. Over portion of individuals with BDD are unmarried, and more than 20% of individuals with body dysmorphia are jobless. Around 20% of individuals with BDD are so upset by their appearance that they endeavor suicide.

In Summary

Assuming you figure you might have BDD, converse with your medical services supplier. They can allude you to a psychological well-being expert who can make a finding involving the measures in the DSM-

Assuming your stresses over your looks are centered more on your body weight or size, you might be determined to have a dietary problem all things considered.

To be determined to have body dysmorphia, the distraction with your appearance should adversely influence your life and additionally cause huge profound pain. Your medical services supplier may likewise indicate whether you have muscle dysmorphia, a kind of body dysmorphia that includes stressing over showing up "excessively little" or not strong enough.

During the indicative cycle, your emotional wellness expert might determine whether you have great or fair understanding into your BDD symptoms.

As indicated by the DSM-5, certain individuals with body dysmorphic jumble have "great" knowledge, and that implies they know that their convictions about their body are false. Individuals with "fair" or "poor" knowledge don't know that their concerns are unreasonable or not situated in reality.

Causes of BDD

The specific reason for body dysmorphia is obscure. Specialists accept that few variables might add to the improvement of BDD, including:

- Hereditary qualities: at times, BDD might be acquired. As per twin examinations, hereditary elements represent around 44% of the difference in body dysmorphic jumble side effects.
- Injury: Individuals with a background marked by injury have a higher possibility creating body dysmorphia. Many individuals with BDD report having been harassed by peers at school, and up to 79% of individuals with body dysmorphia experienced adolescence abuse.
- Character qualities: Individuals with specific character attributes, like hairsplitting and aversion to style, are bound to foster body dysmorphia.
- Comorbid conditions: Many individuals with BDD have undoubtedly another psychological wellness condition simultaneously. It's particularly normal for somebody with body dysmorphia to have OCD, social nervousness problem, or a dietary problem, for example, anorexia nervosa (AN).

Treatment for BDD

Treatment for body dysmorphia as a rule includes psychotherapy (talk treatment) as well as medication.

Experts recommend that the accompanying methodologies are powerful in treating individuals with BDD:

- Mental conduct treatment : Cognitive behavioral therapy can assist individuals with BDD figure out how to deal with their uneasiness and sadness, gain knowledge into their convictions, and fight the temptation to indulge in compulsive ways of behaving.
- Particular serotonin reuptake inhibitors (SSRIs): Studies demonstrate that specific antidepressants, like SSRIs, have been demonstrated to be 53% to 70% viable in treating BDD. Many individuals with body dysmorphia need to take SSRIs on a drawn out premise to lessen their side effects.

Adapting

Assuming you have BDD, it means a lot to fabricate your confidence and connect with others for help. As well as looking for proficient treatment, here are ways to adapt to the side effects of body dysmorphia:

- Joining an online or in-person peer support bunch for individuals with BDD
- Investing energy with friends and family
- Rehearsing care strategies, like contemplation and meditation
- Overseeing pressure with unwinding procedures, for example, profound breathing exercises
- Composing your contemplations in a diary (journaling)
- Utilizing positive certification proclamations to assemble your certainty
- Partaking in another leisure activity or mastering another expertise

CHAPTER FIVE

Body image and beauty standards

As a female, being contrasted with different ladies via web-based entertainment causes the pressure of reasoning that all ladies must have this ideal curve, no cosmetics, and "flawless". Throughout the span of time, ladies have been contrasted with one another, and simply through online entertainment, however in the public eye too. While strolling through the roads while individuals are letting you know that you're neither adequate nor beautiful to the world. This constrains ladies to change their appearance for society's necessities and joys, which can lead them to turning out to be deranged and lose themselves all the while.

The challenges of accepting and valuing yourself as you are

Self-perception is the abstract picture or mental picture of the way that you view yourself actually. It's the manner by which you feel when you thoroughly search in the mirror and look at every one of the bits of yourself, and how you feel about every part of your body.

Beauty standards are grown to a great extent by individuals around us, whether via virtual entertainment or face to face. They are the "rules" (whether composed or unwritten) about how individuals should look or appear in order to be viewed as attractive, pretty or appealing. It's very easy to assimilate the way that society depicts what the ideal body ought to resemble and try your possible best to satisfy those principles.

Media and online entertainment, being shown to us since an early age tells us that we ought to look a specific way, and fit into a specific size. As ladies you are expected to have unrealistic curves and as a man you ought to be excessively muscular and fit.

We put such a lot of torture and pressure on ourselves to depict the "ideal" beauty standards that it can really begin to disintegrate our psychological wellness and the relationship that we have with food. Undesirable food connections can frequently prompt dietary issues which straightforwardly influence actual wellbeing.

Self-perception varies among gender and age ranges. For kids, the way that we handle their responses to their always changing bodies is so significant. Media, sadly, starts placing demands on kids and their appearance from an exceptionally youthful age. This can negatively affect their psychological and actual wellbeing, as well as their self-perception, as youth is a particularly essential time for mental and physical growth and development.

On top of being introduced to the society's beauty standard culture from an early age, these kids also tend to mimic and force this culture to others they meet in school, harassing and bullying others for their looks. The children who face that sort of brutal treatment from their schoolmates at break will frequently take that scar with them all through their lives. This makes them lose their self confidence from such an early stage in their lives.

Even as kids when we were supposed to be taught by our parents and elder ones how to cherish our bodies and love what we put in them, we often heard things like, "would it be a good idea for you to eat that?" or "didn't you just finish eating?". Such statements said over time from such a young age can have adverse effect on our relationship with food later on.

Eating for fuel yet at the same time appreciating what we love with some restraint is too vital to ever be neglected.

Coordinated sports can be another region where positive self-perception could be encouraged by mentors early in life. Nonetheless, this frequently isn't true, truth be told, frequently the inverse is valid.

Young kids who practice in such sports are encouraged to go through extreme measures to keep fit and watch their weight. That can be negative for a little kid who ought to have been figuring out how to cherish and value her body for every one of the superb things it can do.

For youthful grown-ups, especially ladies the assortment of celebrities and influencers that are posted on applications like Instagram might not seem harmful on a normal basis, however they are frequently related with commercials for supplements or fitness routines and exercises, suggesting that we also can have their bodies on the off chance that we just set forth the energy for it. However, that is such a long way from reality. Online entertainment, particularly Instagram, makes it so difficult for people to see these individuals and not question their appearance.

Maybe it would have been better on the off chance that these beauty standards were feasible, yet so many of them, particularly for ladies, depend on altered photographs or restorative medical procedure that attempting to keep up with can be extremely exhausting and overwhelming. For instance, you're to have no hair in any undesirable spots, however ensure that the hair on your head is gleaming and flawless. Ensure you have no fat on your body, besides in the specific perfect spots and in the specific perfect sum. Likewise, you need to ensure you're strong and conditioned, yet all the same not excessively muscular.

While men also face beauty standard pressures, both on the web and in the media, they are totally unique and less extreme, than those faced by ladies. While men are supposed or urged to look a specific way, for ladies it's everything except a prerequisite. The media tosses a great deal more tension on young ladies, and men aren't taken a gander at with such a serious assumption.

For example, the assumptions encompassing body weight frequently fluctuate extensively among people. Overweight men could get prodded, yet they aren't denounced for their bodies being outside the cultural "standard." Larger size ladies anyway are frequently taunted, scorned, and treated as not exactly human. Society has deemed larger size ladies as sluggish, ugly, undesirable, and dishonorable of fundamental regard.

People with larger body sizes are criticized, abused, and mistreated each and every day of their lives. They get loathed on and tortured even by outsiders basically for existing.

Dietary problems spin out of control and are frequently supported. This is seen particularly with plus sized individuals, as society supports being slender regardless of anything else, even over one's wellbeing and security. This is so harming for self-perception, yet mental and actual wellbeing also.

Body size can add to somebody's wellbeing yet isn't demonstrative of it. Society is persuaded that assuming you are slender you are healthy and in the event that you are fat you are not, however that is basically false.

Being slender not minding the fact that you have an unhealthy eating and exercising habit is now deemed healthy than being plus sized whereas you have a healthy eating as exercising habit. Although the reverse should be the case but society does not care the process that results to you being slim as long as you fit into the beauty standards.

There are such countless various individuals out there with such countless novel bodies; it's an insult to set yourself up with these assumptions for seeming to be the supermodels on Instagram or the entertainers on television. As a general rule, everybody's most healthy variant of themselves will be unique to that individual. So rather than agonizing over one's appearance, we ought to fuel our bodies with great food and practicing conventionally through day to day exercises and play.

You should come to acknowledge that regardless of how much exertion you continually place on your body, there are things that won't ever change. Zeroing in on pursuing wellbeing objectives is never something terrible, yet the sooner you arrive at the place of understanding that not all things can be changed and that that is OK, that is the point at which the beauty standards will as of now not make any difference.

More than just dwelling on your appearance alone it is additionally essential to commend your body and what it has done, and can do, for you.

This is all to say that assuming command over your self-perception is vital for carrying on with a blissful and satisfying life.

A positive self-perception implies opportunity; it implies having the option to find a sense of contentment. Attempting to get by in a body that you are repelled by and unnerved to carry with you anyplace is outright torment.

We underestimate our bodies now and then. It is so essential to be sure and wanting to yourself and your body. This body is yours forever; you don't get a subsequent one.

What a Negative Self-perception Means for Psychological well-being

Understanding self-perception, its causes, and its impact permits us to comprehend ways of behaving that are frequently connected with our confidence and self-perception. In some cases, instances of psychological wellness issues are consequences of negative self-perception, for example, anorexia and bulimia nervosa.

We may not be examining the best treatment choices for bulimia nervosa, yet understanding the chance of the body influencing our psychological well-being can break the disgrace in such emotional well-being issues. In the first place, we should attempt to talk about the meaning of self-perception.

What Is Self-perception?

Self-perception is an individual view and feeling towards one's body. Having a sound self-perception implies that you are OK with the manner in which you look and you order your own self-esteem. It likewise incorporates the way of behaving that came about because of those contemplations and sentiments. There's really no need to focus on weight or size. There are individuals who are happy with themselves regardless of not satisfying the ridiculous guidelines of beauty in the public eye.

Be that as it may, there are people who are effortlessly impacted by others' decisions of their appearance, causing them to reprimand themselves and contrast their self-perception and the normally seen self-perception among big names and celebrities or models. Tragically, pictures of such models are most times altered, filtered and depict bogus standards of beauty. Hence, ladies who admire these celebrities will generally find their self-esteem in light of adjusting with the well known ridiculous beauty standards, setting their physical and psychological wellness in danger.

How Society Influences Self-perception?

The chance of fostering a negative self-perception is higher on ladies since young ladies are more compelled to compare severe and ridiculous social beauty standards that are many times centered on the actual characteristics of ladies than whatever else that they are able to do. Acknowledgment of ladies is frequently connected with their appearance regardless of whether they can offer activities, knowledge, and thoughts that are superior to every other person.

This makes ladies helpless against negative self-perception on the grounds that their appearance influences a huge deal about their vocation, achievements, and open doors that can introduce themselves commendable paying little mind to what they look like.

 Ladies, who have positive self-perception, will generally have great psychological well-being conditions. Nonetheless, the pattern in mainstream society and the 'thin ideal' media makes positive self-perception challenging to all ladies as there are different body types that don't fit the 'thin ideal' pattern.

As a result of the overrunning ridiculous beauty standards, ladies are at a higher gamble of experiencing the most widely recognized low confidence to complex issues like dietary problems, gloom, and other adverse consequences on their psychological and actual prosperity. This can likewise prompt more issues in different aspects of their life.

Understanding this connection between the self-perception that famous media presents and its hole from practical self-perceptions can assist us with changing our point of view and manage this issue comprehensively. Assuming society antagonistically influences the strength of the general population, there ought to be endeavors in bringing issues to light about regrettable self-perception, how the disgrace can be broken, and the way in which we can help those impacted by it.

Why bother with beauty standards?

Why order young ladies in light of what they resemble? Indeed, ladies come in various shapes, designs, and tones. Despite the fact that we appear to be unique, in a way we are something similar:

we've all had the battle of society continually passing judgment on you in view of what you resemble and how you are seen via virtual entertainment. However this has occurred throughout the long term, before social media:

- Pre-twentieth century - ideal female body was enticing, rounded midsection, full bosoms and hips
- 1920's - the first part of the primary influx of woman's rights, ladies needing to break with customary standards bound their chests to get the curveless body shape that was all the age
- 1940's-50's - the ideal female body was a stylish housewife with an hourglass figure
- 1960's-70's - the second influx of women's liberation brought back the slender, hermaphroditic body beauty ideal
- 1980's – in this era an ideal beautiful woman was one who was slim but strong
- 1990's - the excellence ideal was a grit stylish, 'whithered stray' look, with ladies who were slight, pale and youthful looking. Huge bosoms began to be famous, and bosom expansion rates in the US soared.

CHAPTER SIX

How your Self-perception affects your Self-Esteem

I'm fat. I'm excessively thin. I'd be blissful on the off chance that I were taller, had wavy hair, straight hair, a more modest nose, greater muscles, longer legs.

Do any of these assertions sound recognizable? Might it be said that you are accustomed to putting yourself down? Provided that this is true, you're in good company. As a human, you're going through a lot of changes in your body. Also, as your body changes, so does your picture of yourself. Bunches of individuals experience difficulty changing, and this can influence their confidence.

Why Are Self-Esteem and Body Image Important?

Confidence is about how much individuals esteem themselves, the pride they feel in themselves, and how beneficial they feel. Confidence is significant in light of the fact that having a decent outlook on yourself can influence how you act. An individual who has high confidence will make companions effectively, is more in charge of their way of behaving, and will appreciate life more.

Self-perception is the way somebody feels about their own actual appearance.

For some individuals, particularly those in their teenage or more youthful years, self-perception can be firmly connected to confidence. That is on the grounds that as children form into adolescents, they care more about how others see them.

What Influences a Person's Self-Esteem?

1. Pubescence

A few teenagers battle with their confidence when they start pubescence in light of the fact that the body goes through many changes. These changes, joined with a characteristic longing to feel acknowledged, mean it tends to be enticing for individuals to contrast themselves as well as other people. They might contrast themselves and individuals around them or with entertainers and celebs they see on TV, in motion pictures, or in magazines.

However, it's difficult to gauge ourselves against others on the grounds that the progressions that accompany adolescence are different for everybody. Certain individuals begin growing early; others are slow developers. Some get an impermanent layer of fat to get ready for growth and others feel like they stay thin regardless of the amount they eat. Everything relies heavily on how our qualities have customized our bodies to act.

The progressions that accompany adolescence can influence how the young ladies and folks feel about themselves. A few young ladies might have an awkward or humiliated outlook on their developing bodies. Others might wish that they were growing quicker. Young ladies might feel strain to be slender however folks might feel as they don't look enormous or healthy.

2. Outside Influences

Numerous different variables (like media pictures ofthin young ladies and built up folks) can influence an individual's self-perception as well.

Day to day life can now and again impact confidence. A few guardians invest more energy reprimanding their children and the manner in which they look than lauding them, which can diminish children's capacity to foster great confidence.

Individuals additionally may encounter negative remarks and destructive prodding about the manner in which they look from schoolmates and companions. At times racial and ethnic bias is the wellspring of such remarks. Albeit these frequently come from obliviousness, here and there they can influence somebody's self-perception and confidence.

3. Solid Self-Esteem

In the event that you have a positive self-perception, you presumably like and acknowledge yourself how you are. This solid disposition permits you to investigate different parts of growing up, like growing great companionships, becoming independent, and testing yourself truly and intellectually. Fostering these pieces of yourself can assist with helping your confidence.

A positive, hopeful mentality can assist individuals with creating solid confidence — for instance, saying, "Hello, I'm human" rather than "Goodness, I'm such a washout" when you've committed an error, or not accusing others when things don't go your way.

Understanding what makes you blissful and how to meet your objectives can assist you with feeling, areas of strength for you to be able to be in charge of your life. An uplifting outlook and a sound way of life (like exercising and eating right) are an extraordinary blend for building great confidence.

Ways to further develop Your Body Image

Certain individuals think they need to change what they look like or act to feel better about themselves. However you should simply have an impact on the manner in which you see your body and your opinion on yourself.

The principal thing to do is perceive that your body is your own, regardless of what shape, size, or variety it comes in. Assuming you're exceptionally stressed over your weight or size, check with your PCP to confirm that things are OK. Be that as it may, it's nobody's business except for your own what your body is like — eventually, you must be content with yourself.

Then, distinguish which parts of your appearance you can reasonably change and which you can't. Everybody (even the absolute best appearing celeb) has things about themselves that they can't change and have to acknowledge — like their height, for instance, or their shoe size.

You can change some things though, (for example, how fit you are), do this by making objectives for yourself. For instance, if you need to get fit, make an arrangement to work-out each day and eat nutritious food varieties. Then, at that point, monitor your advancement until you arrive at your objective. Meeting a test you set for yourself is an incredible method for supporting confidence!

At the point when you hear negative remarks coming from inside yourself, advise yourself to stop. Take a stab at building your confidence by offering yourself three compliments consistently. In the meantime, every night list three things in your day that truly gave you delight. It very well may be anything from the manner in which the sun felt all over, your number one band, or the manner in which somebody chuckled at your jokes. By zeroing in on the beneficial things you do and the good parts of your life, you can change how you feel about yourself.

Where Can I go assuming I Need Help?

Now and then low confidence and self-perception issues are an excessive amount to bear alone. A couple of youngsters might become discouraged, lose interest in exercises or companions — and, surprisingly, hurt themselves or resort to liquor or illicit drug use.

In the event that you're having this impression, it can assist with conversing with a parent, mentor, strict pioneer, life coach, specialist, or a grown-up companion. A trustworthy grown-up — somebody who upholds you and doesn't cut you down — can assist you with putting your self-perception in context and give you certain criticism about your body, your abilities, and your capacities.

In the event that you can't go to anybody you know, call a high schooler emergency hotline (check the business repository under friendly administrations or search on the web). The main thing is to find support assuming you feel like your self-perception and confidence are influencing your life.